Gaming Addiction

Online Addiction
Internet Addiction
How To Overcome Video Game, Internet, And Online Addiction

By Ace McCloud
Copyright © 2013

Disclaimer

The information provided in this book is designed to provide helpful information on the subjects discussed. This book is not meant to be used, nor should it be used, to diagnose or treat any medical condition. For diagnosis or treatment of any medical problem, consult your own physician. The publisher and author are not responsible for any specific health or allergy needs that may require medical supervision and are not liable for any damages or negative consequences from any treatment, action, application or preparation, to any person reading or following the information in this book. Any references included are provided for informational purposes only. Readers should be aware that any websites or links listed in this book may change.

Table of Contents

DEDICATED TO THOSE WHO ARE PLAYING THE GAME OF LIFE TO

WIN

KEEP ON PUSHING AND NEVER GIVE UP!

Ace McCloud

Be sure to check out my website for all my Books and Audio books.

www.AcesEbooks.com

Introduction

I want to thank you and congratulate you for buying the book, "Gaming Addiction: *How To Overcome Video Game Addiction, Internet Addiction, And Online Gaming Addiction*".

Cutting-edge technology in the areas of video games and the internet in general over the last two decades have provided people of all ages, from juveniles to adults, an exciting, entertaining, and extremely engaging way of communicating with each other and passing the time. The exploding popularity of video games and the internet, however, has also given rise to a very serious side effect in the form of addiction. Conservative estimates of the percentage of gaming and internet users that exhibit addictive symptoms hover around ten percent, but most experts agree that since only those who seek professional help are counted, the actual number is much, much higher. Given the severity of the potential consequences of gaming and internet addiction, which include physical, mental, and social risks, it's imperative that parents, family members, friends, etc. be able to identify the warning signs of a loved one who is developing or has already developed a gaming or internet addiction.

This book contains a detailed explanation on how to identify someone who has a video game, internet, or online gaming addiction, and clearly outline the symptoms associated with the condition that any concerned individual should look for. Just as importantly, the book also contains proven steps and strategies on how to assist someone with these addictions, with suggestions ranging from things that can be done at home to providing addicts with an alternative form of entertainment, to seeking professional help.

Chapter 1: An Overview of Gaming and Internet Addiction

Considering that the number of video game players (both on- and off-line) and internet users worldwide is in the billions, gaming and internet addiction is a very serious problem that affects many, many people.

As technology has grown in leaps and bounds, the complexity of video games and the internet has grown exponentially. Graphics have advanced to the point where players feel like they are playing a real-life game. Social media sites allow users to "meet" people from all around the world with the click of a button. Games are designed with more and more levels, so that a player who has invested so much time getting to a certain point feels that they have to continue just so they can make it to the end or keep up with other elite players. The invention of smartphones and tablets has allowed people of all ages to stay online all day long, from any location. The popularity of massive multi-online role-playing games (commonly called MMORPGs) such as "Call of Duty" and "World of Warcraft" provide players with a game that never really ends, as the user has millions of play options and the content is continually being updated. In short, the people who develop games and websites are very good at what they do. Their goal is to hook users into spending as much time as possible playing a certain game or interacting with a certain site. And while their incredible success is great for the companies producing these forms of entertainment, it spells trouble for individuals who go on to develop gaming and internet addictions, spending hours on end in front of TV's and monitors.

According to experts, for a condition to become an addiction, the following two criteria must be met. First, a user must feel that in order to be able to carry on, they must have more of a substance or behavior (in this case, playing video games or using the internet). Secondly, if a person is denied access to their particular substance or addiction, they immediately become noticeably irritated, angry, depressed, etc. If not dealt with, either in the early stages or at a later point, the addiction can cause long-lasting physical and social damage to the afflicted individual.

Chapter 2: Physical Risks of Gaming and Internet Addiction

Physically, an addicted gamer or internet user may experience a host of issues, carpal tunnel syndrome being one of them. This condition develops when the primary nerve that runs between the hand and forearm is pinched or squeezed. For quite some time now, carpal tunnel syndrome has been linked to prolonged computer use, since repetitive actions like clicking a mouse, moving a joystick, and pressing buttons, can inflame the carpal tunnel area of the wrist where the main nerve is located. This can cause pain in various parts of the hand.

Another physical ailment that can be caused by gaming addiction is headaches and migraines (excessively painful headaches.) Migraine headaches generally can first be felt in only one location, but then little by little, spread to other areas of the head, and as they do so, become more and more painful. To someone who is experiencing a migraine, things such as light and noise can multiply the pain several fold. In extremely severe cases, a migraine can even cause someone to begin vomiting. Because of the long periods of concentration and straining of the eyes that gamers go through, they are more at risk for suffering from headaches and migraines.

Given that addictions can cause people to ignore their bodies signals of needing sleep, gamers experience very high rates of sleep-related disorders such as sleep apnea, insomnia, narcolepsy, nocturnal myoclonus (which is the fidgeting of the arms and/or legs during sleep), and parasomnia (which can include anything from simple nightmares and night terrors to sleepwalking or talking). This population seems to be more prone to sleep-disorders because the disorders are partially caused by overstimulation of the brain, which excessive gaming can do. But obsessively thinking about a certain game or website can also lead to sleep-related disorders.

Since playing video games and using the internet are more often than not sedentary activities which keep people sitting in the same position for hours and hours at a time, it follows that gaming addicts are at a high risk of back problems. It is easy for nerves to get compressed over the years, even leading to herniated discs in the lower back or even the neck area if proper posture isn't being used along with frequent breaks. While some back problems take years before they develop into serious health problems, in the short term users can experience stiff, cramped, and sore backs as well as necks.

Eating disorders are very common amongst the gaming addict community. When fully consumed by a game or website, users tend to choose their food items based on what is fastest to prepare, choosing quick, premade, processed items over healthier ones that might require a larger time investment to cook. Over the long term, a person denying their body essential nutritional items (or food in general if they are simply skipping meals) can lead to an array of diet-related disorders.

Hand in hand with sleeping disorders, eating disorders, and back and neck problems, addicts put themselves at a higher risk of becoming obese simply because they are stationary for so long. Time that could be spent being physically active is instead spent sitting in front of a screen for great lengths of time, which can lead to weight gain, especially if they are not exercising. Coupled with the previous ailments mentioned, obesity can cause some very serious short-term and long-term health complications for those who suffer from it.

Finally, personal hygiene may suffer if someone becomes addicted enough to gaming. Performing self-cleanliness tasks such as bathing, brushing and flossing teeth, shaving, etc. get pushed to the side, as satisfying the addiction becomes the person's main priority. Letting oneself go hygiene-wise can quickly become noticeable and intolerable in social settings such as at school and work, where the user may still have to go on a regular basis. If they already were experiencing low self-esteem and isolation from social groups, their deteriorating hygiene will only subject them to further scrutiny and possibly ridicule.

Chapter 3: Social Risks of Gaming and Internet Addiction

While the physical consequences of developing a video game or internet addiction may be easier to spot right away (in the form of sudden weight gain or deteriorating hygiene), the developmental consequences can remain hidden for months and even years without being detected. Yet in the long run, a user can cause themselves more irreparable harm through stunted personal growth than through their physical maladies.

Often times, the isolation of video games or the internet is what appeals to users who eventually become addicted. They may already be overweight, socially awkward, have low self-esteem, etc., and grow tired of constantly feeling rejected in social situations that present themselves either at school or work. To them, it is much easier to interact with a game or a website that is built to let anyone in, versus a society that so often screens people based on appearance, wealth, education, status, etc. Their isolation from others becomes even deeper, then, as the addiction becomes self-reinforcing.

For those on the fringe of having healthy friendships and sexual relationships, being addicted can put a serious strain on those relationships. In extreme cases, developing a gaming or internet addiction can lead people to completely ignore their spouse, choosing instead to spend their time alone in front of the screen rather than eating with them, talking with them, even having sex with them. They become so obsessed by their addiction that they put aside the person that had up until now brought them an infinite amount of happiness.

More commonly, however, a person simply begins to ignore their friends, preferring instead to play games or surf the web on their own. The change may take a while to become noticeable, but soon enough a user may start ignoring calls at typically social times of the week (such as the late afternoons, Friday nights, or weekends).

Sacrificing friendships and intimate relationships is harmful for adults, but for children and adolescents, it is especially bad. The adolescent and teenage years (precisely the years where these addictions seem to take hold the strongest) are an extremely important time for young adults developmentally. They are years where children need lots of practice interacting with all types of people in varied social settings, so that once they get older, they have plenty of experience functioning in society and controlling their emotions at the same time. Also, it is a chance for kids to surround themselves with a strong, solid support system of people they feel comfortable sharing their feelings with, and that they can pass through life with having shared common experiences. When adolescents "miss" part of their youth experience because they were alone in a room playing games or on the web, they may wake up years later and find themselves feeling partially empty because they did not solidify those long-lasting friendships that the school years tend to offer. Additionally, they may feel inept in certain social situations, whether it be at work, college, the military, etc. because they removed themselves from so many social situations as a kid and did not give themselves the opportunity to practice interacting with both other children and adults, preferring instead to be online or playing video games.

While parents may become extremely frustrated by the deteriorating academic achievement of their child, ultimately the low grades and disinterest in learning will have long term consequences as the child gets older.

Perhaps they will be denied admission to a university of their choice, or be turned away from studying a certain major of their liking. Once they are done with school, they may have to settle for a less desirable first job, since they don't have the degree or experience that they would have had if they had focused more on their studies. From there on, they will always find themselves a bit behind where they should have been career-wise because their addiction got the best of them as an adolescent.

The harmful physical consequences of gaming addiction can also lead to social consequences. Weight gain can cause a child to not perform as well on the athletic field, possibly leading them to lose interest in the sport for a bit or leaving it altogether. Lack of hygiene can bring about much unwanted scrutiny for an adult at work. Carpal tunnel syndrome can force someone to take some time off from the job, in the process causing them to miss certain promotions. A sleeping disorder has many consequences, one of which is keeping someone away from the bedroom at night, a time which couples tend to value because it gives them time alone to focus on each other, since during the day there are often so many other items to attend to. On the other hand, an addiction may exhaust someone to the point that they don't have the energy to put into being intimate with their significant other, which in turn can put a serious strain on the relationship. The consequences of a gaming addiction, in many ways, can contribute to an overall lower quality of life for the person involved.

Because the physical and developmental risks of gaming and internet addictions can be so harmful, it is imperative that people who develop the condition have a strong, caring group of friends and family around them that can not only identify the warning signs of the addiction, but also put into place measures that will help the addict break free from the grasp that the addiction has over them.

Chapter 4: Identifying the Warning Signs of Gaming and Internet Addiction

While most people probably associate a gaming or internet addiction with socially awkward teenage boys, the condition can afflict people of all ages and gender. The warning signs are universal, regardless of what stage the user may be at in life. And even a user who exhibits only one or two symptoms can still be considered addicted.

One of the first indications that let family and friends of an addict know there might be a problem is an obsessive preoccupation with a game or website. When someone develops a gaming addiction, it can consume their every thought, and not just when they are actually playing or using the site. Addicts will think and talk about the game all the time, not listening to others during conversation to the point where it may become extremely intolerable to be around them. In the worst cases, addicts will continue to bring up the game or website during the most inappropriate times, such as during class or at a work meeting.

Users who become addicted oftentimes tend to downplay the amount of time they spend gaming or online. As with addictions of any nature, a strong sense of denial can take hold within the addict. If the addiction grows worse and the user senses that more and more people are confronting them over it, the fierceness of the denials may grow, as the user may feel cornered or that all of his friends and family are ganging up on them for no justifiable reason. It's also not uncommon for both child and adult addicts to outright lie about how much time they are spending playing games or being online. They do so in the hopes that both their friends and family will drop the subject and not try and restrict their play, while also trying to convince themselves that they are fine.

Addicts may soon experience a lack of control over how much time they spend on their addiction. Even well-meaning individuals who intend to only spend ten or fifteen minutes playing games or being online can soon "wake up" hours later, realizing that they have spent the entire day or night in front of the screen. An addiction that has taken complete control over an individual can render even an aware individual helpless. They may know that they have a problem and admit it to themselves and others, yet they cannot control it and find themselves unable to stop.

Sadly, other areas of an addict's life may soon begin to suffer because of the addiction. Homework and studying may be ignored, causing grades to fall. Work projects and meetings go ignored, causing work performance to deteriorate. Hygiene becomes an afterthought, causing others to scrutinize the lack of bathing, shaving, or clean clothes, all characteristic of someone who seems to have forgotten some basic social norms that people without a disorder willingly follow. Even friends and family may notice that their loved one is growing distant, choosing to spend their days and nights alone in front of the screen instead of interacting with them, as they previously used to enjoy doing. In the most extreme cases, a person may altogether withdraw from social settings, skipping school or work, quitting sports teams, ignoring spouses and children, etc., seemingly content to sit alone and play or be online.

Addicts may also use their gaming or internet addiction as a way to self-medicate from problems in their lives. In the same way that alcoholics "drink away the pain," gaming and internet addicts prefer to retreat back into the virtual world contained within the screen instead of dealing with their real-life issues. This is especially true for users who experience bouts of intense sadness, anger, and self-doubt, triggered by a problematic sexual relationship, an argument with a friend, or a poor test grade, for example. Instead of confronting the root cause of their emotion, they choose avoidance.

For adults especially, the misuse of money is often a very clear indicator that an addiction has taken hold. Video games, online gambling, etc. are not cheap hobbies, and bills can quickly run up into the thousands, as a user feels they need to keep up with the latest equipment. With gambling especially, there is no limit as to how much an addict can lose. In the most extreme cases, adults have driven themselves into bankruptcy to fuel their gambling addiction, causing untold stress on their families in the process. Since teens do not have as much disposable income as an adult who works full-time, the financial damage caused by the addiction is usually not as bad. But an addiction in young adults is just as powerful as in adults, and if they are short on cash, friends and family members should be on the lookout, as an addicted teen may soon start to steal from those around them to keep their addiction going. Even necessary purchases such as groceries, utility bills, school supplies, etc. may be put to the side so that the addict's disposable income can go towards supporting their addiction.

A lot of times, a user may even be aware that they are seeking short-term pleasure through their game or internet time at the expense of more meaningful personal interactions with friends and family. After some time, they may feel guilty that they spend so much time playing or surfing the web, yet they cannot deny themselves that sense of euphoria they feel from being in front of the screen.

Most obvious of all are the physical signs that someone has become addicted to gaming or the internet. They may develop sleeping disorders which can keep them up all night long and prevent them from getting a good night's rest. They may develop bags under their eyes. Their back may be achy from sitting for great periods of time, or their wrist and hands may hurt from the carpal tunnel syndrome they have developed. They let themselves go appearance-wise, skipping showers, not shaving, not brushing their hair or their teeth, or not exercising to the point where their body begins to become noticeably heavier. If physical warning signs such as these are present, family and friends should become concerned that the person they care about has developed an addiction.

While the previous list is by no means exhaustive, it can provide concerned friends and family with some key symptoms to look for in a person with a possible gaming or internet addiction. And again, a user need not exhibit all the warning signs. Even one or two of the previously mentioned behaviors is enough to let concerned individuals know that the person they love may have a problem.

Chapter 5: Help With Gaming and Internet Addiction

Once a gaming or internet addiction has been identified in an individual, there are several courses of action family and friends can take to assist that person to break free from their condition. Unfortunately, given that technology is so prevalent in our modern everyday lives (both at school and at work), it is unrealistic to think that an individual can be prevented from being in front of a screen at all times throughout the course of their day. Parents may have a bit more authoritative power to lock up a gaming console or computer at home, versus, say, a wife trying to deal with her husband's addiction. But unless parents can provide constant supervision for their child, children will always find a way to undermine their parents wishes. They can play games on their phone both during and after school. They can sneak over to a friend's house and fuel their addiction there. They can wake up in the middle of the night when their parents are sleeping. Controlling an addict's exposure to gaming or computer equipment is simply not a viable, easily enforceable option. There are, however, much more effective strategies to deal with gaming and internet addictions.

The first thing family and friends need to do is confront the individual. Large group interventions often put the addict on the defensive, so perhaps only one or two people need to be present. For a child or teenager, a parent could raise the issue with their child. For an adult, a spouse might want to ask a close friend to be present, or even to bring the issue up on their own. Sometimes an individual can become resentful if a spouse tries to talk to them about having a gaming addiction, as they might feel that they are simply trying to control them.

Having someone outside the marriage or relationship might ease that tension a bit. If the intervener is at a loss for words on how to approach the issue, they should take a direct approach and show them some literature on gaming and internet addictions. Together, they can read over the warning signs and consequences of the addiction, with the intervener asking the addict if they see any of those symptoms in themselves. Hopefully, the addict will admit that they do have a problem, but more often than not, their embarrassment, shame, or pride will keep them denying it until the bitter end. At this point, just be honest with them, remembering to not get angry, excited, or condescending, but simply telling them which of the symptoms you've seen in them, and providing them with specific examples. If, however, even while talking one-on-one with a loved one the addict becomes defensive and begins to close off, the intervener should steer the conversation away from the specific addiction and instead just tell the addict how much they mean to them, how important they are in their lives, how much they miss spending time with them, and how upsetting it is to see them become more and more distant with each passing day.

More often than not, an individual turns to excessive gaming or internet use because they are suffering quietly from some other issue in their life. It may be financial hardship. It may be feelings of social isolation at school or at work. It may be a deteriorating marriage. Whatever the case may be, addicts are most likely trying to escape from their real-world problems by immersing themselves in a virtual world that they have complete control over, which is a very appealing concept, especially to shy and socially awkward teenage boys. The discussion should try to get to the bottom of what's bothering the afflicted individual.

Once the addict realizes that this certain (or several issues) is causing them to turn to gaming excessively, some possible solutions can be offered. A socially insecure teenager, for example, will need to be provided with opportunities to interact with other teens face-to-face, in a safe, secure environment. A parent or friend can look into after-school clubs for the addict which center around something that might interest them. There are even retreats and summer camps that are geared towards getting socially inept kids to open up a bit and work on their social skills and overall confidence. This usually involves plenty of outdoors, confidence-building, non-competitive activities. Sports teams and military-style boot camps are also an option, but tend to be very competitive places filled with alpha male-type kids constantly measuring each other up; exactly the type of place that a gamer or internet user would hate.

The easiest way to help an addict get over their addiction is to help them find another activity that they can spend time working on. If a child has an artistic side, let them redesign their room. If they enjoy working with their hands, let them do some carpentry or pottery. If they are the creative type, encourage them to work on some fictional short stories, maybe even taking them around to some writers workshops to submit their own writing.

Parents should also include their children in the decision-making process with regards to setting reasonable game and internet usage times. It's important for the child to have some input so that they can understand why a reasonable number of hours needs to be set, with priority given to schoolwork and other physical and intellectual pursuits. But also, it's always easier to get children to follow rules if they themselves have helped in creating them.

And while it may be tempting to pile on extra chores so as to keep an addict too busy to play, the feeling of being punished may turn the child off from trying to break free from the addiction.

An addicted adult should also find something that can pique their interest so that they can begin to turn away from gaming or the internet. Reading is a great alternative. It is also wise to note that an addicted adult will often times need emotional support from friends and family to get them to follow through with the healing process.

There are also some alternative treatments addicts can consider trying in conjunction with or apart from the treatments mentioned above. Some of the treatments include hypnosis, herbal/supplement therapy, acupuncture, homeopathy, aromatherapy, chiropractic, and religion, to name a few. There have been plenty of documented cases showing addicts quitting their gaming and internet addictions shortly after undergoing an alternative treatment. Users should be reminded, however, that the medical community generally does not endorse such treatments because of the lack of concrete scientific evidence supporting their healing ability.

It is also a good idea for the addicted person to make a list of goals that they want to accomplish in the short-term, the mid-term, and the long-term. The goals can be anything they want to accomplish in life. After making the goals, they should seriously review them and ask themselves if they can accomplish these goals while spending the majority of their time and energy in front of a tv or monitor. In most cases the answer is no, so then they should make a chart that splits up their time in a proportional manner so that it is possible to accomplish their goals. This will let them plainly see how they need to spend their time in order to have a more successful life. A person does not necessarily need to quit their preferred activity, but it should be limited to just one or two hours a day, using the rest of their time to focus on their chosen short-term, mid-term, and long-term goals.

Visualization is also very helpful. The addicted person should visualize themselves working on, acting on, and accomplishing their new goals. They need to realize that by making some more intelligent decisions, they can enjoy a much more fulfilling life, and still devote a few hours a day to their favorite activity if desired. They should visualization themselves succeeding at their life goals. On the other hand, they should also visualize their life if they continue to spend it the way they are, with countless hours spent in front of a screen. The negative consequences should be brought to the mind, and hopefully a sense of urgency will develop to improve their life for the better and start living it in more intelligent and fulfilling ways.

It is also good idea to use the particular addiction as a reward. So, maybe no playing video games until later on in the day when everything else has been accomplished. If you are too busy to get the basics accomplished, then you are definitely too busy to be wasting your time and energy in front of a screen.

Nothing feels as good as being fit and healthy. One of the greatest cures for nearly any type of addiction is a healthy diet and good exercise every day. It is amazing how things can change for the better when you are eating and exercising properly. There are countless books on health and nutrition. It is highly recommended that a daily exercise routine be taken up, even if it's only walking, and that fresh fruits and vegetables are a part of your everyday diet.

If you have the willpower or the desire to truly be rid of your addiction, then many times there is only one action to take. This is to actually sell, throw away, or delete the addicting game or machine. I was personally addicted to World of Warcraft, and played it for many years, actually getting to the point of being a world top 100 player (out of 20 million people). I played the game between six and twelve hours a day for close to two years straight. When I finally had the ultimate character and all the items and all the gold, and nearly everything done in the game, it was then that I realized it wasn't as fulfilling as I thought it would be. After several months of being a top player, it actually got to be a bit boring, and the game seemed more like a job than fun anymore. I finally came to the realization that my real life was suffering way too much just so I could be a pro player, and that feeling at the top of utter joy was gone soon enough.

It wasn't until I sold my character and deleted the game from my computer that I was finally able to put the game to rest and start focusing on more important aspects of my life. It's at that point that I truly started to make big improvements. It took me a year to get back into decent physical condition after I quit gaming seriously, and I still have recurring neck, back, and hand problems from all my years of hardcore gaming. But the good news is, it's amazing how much energy you will have for other things when you start focusing that time and energy on your life and your health as a priority! If you have hand pain or arm pain then I would highly recommend my book on Carpal Tunnel Syndrome.

Now, I haven't quit gaming all together, but I have made some changes that make it more of an asset than a liability. One major change I made was that I stopped playing games on the computer. As I do most of my work at the computer, playing video games at the computer was only extending my time in the same position for hours at a time. I now play games on the play station, in a lazy boy recliner (which has much less stress on my lower back and neck), and I only play for 15-30 minutes at a time. I also only try to play after all my other work is accomplished, and I only choose games that I can pause or save at any time. After 15-30 minutes, I will either turn off the game, or I will pause it to do something else productive, maybe to stretch or just go outside for some fresh air, and then continue the game a bit later on after doing a few more productive things.

The thrill of a new game or being online is very exciting, and not necessarily something that needs to be totally abolished from your life, if you can be disciplined. There are also some benefits to gaming, including increased hand eye coordination, increased cognitive function, and there even have been studies done that say gaming may decrease the chances of a person getting Alzheimer's disease. Every person is different, however, so it is best to choose the strategy that works best for you and stick to it. As mentioned earlier, the long term effects of gaming and being online for most of the day, months at a time, can be quite devastating.

As with any addiction, the road to recovery is always full of twists and turns. It will likely be an uphill struggle, for all parties involved, with both big and small relapses along the way. It's important to keep in mind that this is to be expected, and to not give up hope. Knowing that there are loved ones around them that are very concerned is often the only thing that can keep an addict on the road to recovery, even if at times it seems like they are not doing their part to change their behavior. If the situation becomes desperate, professional help can and should be sought. There are trained professionals that specialize in treating children and adults that have developed gaming and internet addictions, and while they may be costly, the cost of doing nothing to help the addicted individual will be far greater in the long run.

Conclusion

I hope this book was able to help you better understand the warning signs of gaming and internet addiction, and what to do if you or someone you know is addicted. Be sure to use the techniques and suggestions that work the best for you, and remember that life is more enjoyable in moderation, and that there is much more things to do in life than to sit in front of a video screen. Making your health the number one priority is a habit that will keep you happy, healthy and strong throughout your life.

Finally, if you discovered at least one thing that has helped you or that you think would be beneficial to someone else, be sure to take a few seconds to easily post a quick positive review. As an author, your positive feedback is desperately needed. Your highly valuable five star reviews are like a river of golden joy flowing through a sunny forest of mighty trees and beautiful flowers! *To do your good deed in making the world a better place by helping others with your valuable insight, just leave a nice review.*

My Other Books and Audio Books

www.AcesEbooks.com

Peak Performance Books

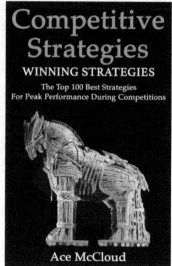

Health Books

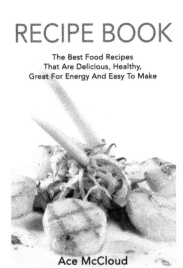

RECIPE BOOK

The Best Food Recipes
That Are Delicious, Healthy,
Great For Energy And Easy To Make

Ace McCloud

MASSAGE THERAPY

TRIGGER POINT THERAPY
ACUPRESSURE THERAPY
Learn The Best Techniques For
Optimum Pain Relief And Relaxation

Ace McCloud

LOSE WEIGHT

THE TOP 100 BEST WAYS
TO LOSE WEIGHT QUICKLY AND HEALTHILY

Ace McCloud

FATIGUE
OVERCOME CHRONIC FATIGUE

Discover How To Energize
Your Body & Mind So
That You Can Bring
The Energy & Passion
Back Into Your Life

Ace McCloud

Be sure to check out my audio books as well!

Happiness
The Top 100 Best Ways
To Feel Good & Be Happy

Ace McCloud

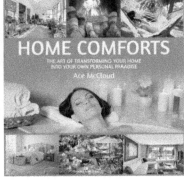

HOME COMFORTS
THE ART OF TRANSFORMING YOUR HOME
INTO YOUR OWN PERSONAL PARADISE
Ace McCloud

MOTIVATION
MASTER THE POWER OF MOTIVATION
TO PROPEL YOURSELF TO SUCCESS

Ace McCloud

Check out my website at: **www.AcesEbooks.com** for a complete list of all of my books and high quality audio books. I enjoy bringing you the best knowledge in the world and wish you the best in using this information to make your journey through life better and more enjoyable! **Best of luck to you!**

www.ingramcontent.com/pod-product-compliance
Lightning Source LLC
Chambersburg PA
CBHW060109090326
40690CB00063B/4351